Date Due

PERGAMON INTERNATIONAL LIBRARY
of Science, Technology, Engineering and Social Studies

The 1000-volume original paperback library in aid of education,
industrial training and the enjoyment of leisure

Publisher: Robert Maxwell, M.C.

The Japanese Approach to Product Quality

Its Applicability to the West

A Related Journal

OMEGA

The International Journal of Management Science*

Chief Editor: Samuel Eilon, Imperial College of Science and Technology, London

OMEGA provides all specialists in management science with important new developments in operational research and managerial economics. Published material ranges from original contributions to review articles describing the state-of-the-art in specific areas, together with shorter critical assessment of particular management techniques.

*Free specimen copy available on request

The Japanese Approach to Product Quality

Its Applicability to the West

Edited by

NAOTO SASAKI

Professor of Economics and Industrial Administration, Sophia University, Japan

and

DAVID HUTCHINS

David Hutchins Associates, UK

PERGAMON PRESS

OXFORD · NEW YORK · TORONTO · SYDNEY · PARIS · FRANKFURT

U.K.	Pergamon Press Ltd., Headington Hill Hall, Oxford OX3 0BW, England
U.S.A.	Pergamon Press Inc., Maxwell House, Fairview Park, Elmsford, New York 10523, U.S.A.
CANADA	Pergamon Press Canada Ltd., Suite 104, 150 Consumers Rd., Willowdale, Ontario M2J 1P9, Canada
AUSTRALIA	Pergamon Press (Aust.) Pty. Ltd., P.O. Box 544, Potts Point, N.S.W. 2011, Australia
FRANCE	Pergamon Press SARL, 24 rue des Ecoles, 75240 Paris, Cedex 05, France
FEDERAL REPUBLIC OF GERMANY	Pergamon Press GmbH, Hammerweg 6, D-6242 Kronberg-Taunus, Federal Republic of Germany

First edition 1984

Library of Congress Cataloging in Publication Data

Main entry under title:
The Japanese approach to product quality.
"Collection of papers presented to the past four conferences of QC circle held in London since 1976" ——P.
Bibliography: p.
1. Quality circles — Addresses, essays, lectures.
2. Quality control — Japan — Addresses, essays, lectures.
I. Sasaki, Naoto, 1936—   . II. Hutchins, David C.
HD66.J36 1983   658.4'036   83-13154

British Library Cataloguing in Publication Data

The Japanese approach to product quality.
1. Quality circles — Japan
I. Sasaki, Naoto   II. Hutchins, David
670'.68'4   HD66

ISBN 0-08-028159-1 (Hardcover)
ISBN 0-08-028160-5 (Flexicover)

Printed and bound in Great Britain by
William Clowes Limited, Beccles and London

Preface

In recent years the quality of Japanese products has been a focus of world attention and perhaps has been the main cause of the so-called "trade imbalance" between Japan and other countries. But no matter how good the quality or how strong the Japanese economy, it is impossible to force consumers in other countries to buy Japanese products: they have "consumers' sovereignty". Although the quality of Japanese products is good, if their price were much higher they would not sell so well. To state the matter simply, the combination of quality and price must be linked with high productivity, taking into account the fact that Japanese workers are no longer suppliers of "cheap labour".

Good quality and high productivity, however, have been thought, especially in the West, to be a contradiction in terms. In Japan these two factors have had a high correlation since 1950's "cheap and bad" products have been transformed into reliable ones, although the Japanese are not as yet impressively innovative.

What is innovative in Japan may not necessarily be found in the products themselves, but in the production process. In other words, what Japanese manufacturers have achieved so far is *process* innovation rather than product innovation. It is vitally important to notice that human factors have a greater influence on the former than on the latter. Product innovation can be made up of the "1 per cent inspiration" of geniuses, but process innovation can only be realized by the "99 per cent perspiration" of co-operative work forces. Put another way, it must, to a greater or lesser extent, result from innovation in the human system on the shop floor. In this respect, Japanese manufacturers seem to have made their impact.

The QC Circle is a crystallization of that style of process innovation which is a small-group activity in which workers apply basic tools of statistical quality control to their own work on the shop floor. Although the details of this will be left to future chapters, at least one thing should be clearly noted in the first place. That is the fact we have already passed the stage of discussing whether it is possible to transplant the QC Circle from Japan to other countries. We now find cases of its success across countries regardless of cultural differences.

This book is a collection of papers presented to the past four conferences of QC Circle held in London since 1979. But this is not just a mere collection. The papers have been arranged into a particular order and edited by two people, one of whom, David Hutchins, organized the conferences and the other, Naoto Sasaki, chaired them. They were edited in order to avoid too much overlap and are linked with each other by editorial commentaries. Also included are papers from Mullard and Wedgwood who have subsequently made encouraging progress with the introduction of the concept in their organizations.

Concerning the name "Quality Control Circle", there is a variety of names already in existence in the world for this concept. In most cases, it is called either QC Circle or Quality Circle. In the latter case, the word Control has been dropped because it has been thought to sound oppressive or suppressive. In this book we have respected the preference of contributors.

The editors are especially grateful to Professor Kaoru Ishikawa, who is known as the "Father of QC Circles" and who is now the President of the Musashi Institute of Technology in Tokyo, for his excellent help to the first QC Circle conference held in London in September 1979 by giving a full-day speech, and also for his kind permission for this book to include the contents of that speech.

They are also greatly indebted to the speakers at the conferences and to the contributors of the papers, as well as to the Union of Japanese Scientists and Engineers (JUSE), the headquarters of QC Circle, for the birth of this book. But it goes without saying that the editors are responsible for any possible errors or misunderstandings in this book.

The editors also give their warm appreciation to Miss Naoko Muramatsu, a student of Sophia University, for her great effort and help in typing all the disorderly drafts into a completely orderly manuscript.

NAOTO SASAKI
DAVID HUTCHINS

Contents

Contents

List of Figures

1

Quality Control in Japan

KAORU ISHIKAWA

President, Musashi Institute of Technology

1. Its Brief History

Before the end of World War II there was little application of statistical quality control (SQC) in Japan. Its introductory period was from 1946 to 1950. At first, it was introduced from the United States, by the U.S. Army, and particularly by Dr. W. E. Deming, and also through a number of books. In 1948, a QC Research Group was organized in the Union of Japanese Scientists and Engineers (JUSE). The members of this group were university professors in the fields of engineering and statistics; government officers, and engineers from private companies. In 1949 JUSE initiated a long QC Seminar, named the QC Basic Course.

The years 1951–1954 saw the further development of SQC, and the Deming Prize was established in 1951. In this period various QC methods developed and many good results were achieved, although there remained three major defects:

(a) There was too much tendency towards statistical methods.
(b) Standardization was promoted, but with rather too much formality.
(c) Top management lagged behind in the progress.

Around that time, in 1954, Dr. J. M. Juran was invited from the USA and he emphasized that QC should be conducted as an integral part of management control. Following this, in the years 1955–1960, the Company Wide Quality Control (CWQC) movement started. And now, when one company wants to apply CWQC, all the employees, from top management to foremen and workers, study statistical methods and participate in QC. And in 1962, publication of a magazine, *Genba-To-QC* (*QC for the Foremen*) commenced, and "QC Circles" were organized in various factories.

Over the years the quality of products and Quality Control itself have made remarkable progress in Japan.

1

2. Features of Quality Control in Japan

2.1. *Company-wide QC – CWQC*

QC in Japan is characterized by company-wide participation, from top management to the lower-ranking employees. It is an activity participated in not only by the departments of technology, design, research and manufacturing but also sales, materials and clerical or management departments such as planning, accounting, business and personnel. QC concepts and methods are used for solving problems in the production process, for incoming material control and new product design control, and also for analyses to help top management decide on company policy, for checking if top management's policy is being carried out, for solving problems in sales activities, for personnel and labour management, and for solving problems in clerical departments.

The results of these company-wide QC activities are remarkable, not only in ensuring the quality of industrial products but also in their great contribution to the company's overall business.

2.2. *QC Audit by Top Management*

The QC Audit is carried out by a team of top management, headed by the president of the company, who visit each plant, sales office and department to investigate the degree to which their company policies and QC programs are being carried out, and to eliminate any obstacle which might hinder them. The head of each department carries out a QC Audit in his own department. Furthermore, QC Audits are carried out for affiliated companies and suppliers of raw materials and parts.

2.3. *Means of Recognition from Outside*

The Deming Prize was established in 1951 to commemorate the friendship and achievements of Dr. W. E. Deming. It consists of two different awards, the Deming Prize and the Prize for Application, which are awarded to individuals or companies after examination by the Deming Prize Committee. This committee is not governmental. The award is considered to be the most distinguished QC award and there are many companies which make the Prize their first goal in their efforts for the promotion of QC. The Prize plays a major role in the promotion of QC, SQC and CWQC in Japan.

2.4. JIS (Japanese Industrial Standard) Certification Mark

Another means of outside recognition is the Japanese Industrial Standard (JIS) Certification Mark, which gives a national guarantee of quality to Japanese products. All good products bear the "JIS" mark, whether they come from small, middle or large enterprises. To be eligible for "JIS" approval, a company must practice SQC. The "JIS" mark may be given only after certain conditions are satisfied, and after investigations on the state of SQC application are made.

Although this system is effective in promoting QC in Japan, there are some problems, because most of the governmental QC specialists have only a theoretical knowledge of SQC concept and methods from the literature and have no experience of it in practice. In such a case, QC can easily become a formal, or "document", QC.

2.5. Industrial Education and Training

In order for company-wide QC to be applied we must educate every employee, from the top ranking to the bottom. Through education and training each employee displays his capability to the full, and eventually his infinite possibilities are drawn out. But such an industrial education and training system also has its weakness: it takes too much time to develop. In the case of a large company, it may take more than three years to disseminate fully CWQC.

2.6. QC Circle Activities

One major characteristic of Japanese company-wide QC is the QC circle movement, started in 1962. A QC circle is a group of from 5 to 10 workers. The leader may be a foreman, assistant foreman, work leader, or one of the workers.

The circle leader and members, having mastered SQC statistical methods, utilize them to improve quality and operation standards and achieve significant results in quality improvement, cost reduction, productivity and safety. Statistical methods are frequently applied in Japan, and through education and training in SQC methods all of the employees become able to use the so-called *seven tools* (1, Pareto charts; 2, cause & effects diagrams; 3, stratification; 4, check sheets; 5, histograms; 6, scatter diagrams; 7, Shewharts control charts & graph). Many of the Japanese QC engineers find the complicated statistical methods to their natural taste.

2.7. *Nation-wide QC Promotion Activities*

In Japan the core of QC promotion is made up of private organizations such as JUSE (Union of Japanese Scientists and Engineers) and JSA (Japanese Standards Association), rather than governmental QC promotion bodies.

Each November various "Quality Month" events are held, sponsored by these organizations and with the support of the government Ministries. These events are part of the Nation-wide QC promotion activities and every May the QC Regional Conference for QC Staff and Middle Management is held in different major cities each year on a rota basis.

Furthermore, QC Circle Conferences are held about 80 times a year all over the country. The number of persons attending these conferences and meetings in 1976 was more than 60 000. On these occasions, presentations of QC Circles and plant tours are made.

Every October is "Standardization Promotion Month", and the General Meeting of Standardization is held. These nation-wide QC promotion activities are a major force in the QC movement in Japan.

The members of the committees for most of these nation-wide quality control promotion activities are volunteers from the QC research group. JUSE and JSA back up these committees, but financially the committees are managed on a self-payment basis.

3. Definition of Quality Control in Japan

Some people are under the misapprehension that QC is just the manufacturing of goods to the best quality. However, the meaning of quality in QC is that which satisfies the customer and not only what satisfies National Standards. QC means to design, to produce, and to sell goods which actually meet the needs of the user. Good quality means quality which is produced with the maximum use of the manufacturer's existing capability such as production, engineering and process capability to meet consumer needs.

Statistical methods have been applied extensively to QC in Japan, especially since the end of World War II. But this statistical quality control (SQC) has been developed in Japan to become a broader concept called company-wide quality control (CWQC), where quality means not only quality of product but also of after-sales service, quality of management, the company itself and the human being. There all departments, including top management, must coordinate their activities to participate in promoting QC.

The effects derived from realizing this definition are as follows:
1. Product quality is improved and becomes uniform. Defects are reduced; 2. Reliability of goods is improved; 3. Cost is reduced; 4. Quantity of production is increased, and it becomes possible to make rational production schedules; 5. Wasteful work and rework are reduced; 6. Technique is established and improved; 7. Expenses for inspection and testing are reduced; 8. Contracts between vendor and vendee are rationalized; 9. The sales market is enlarged; 10. Better relationships are established among departments; 11. False data and reports are reduced; 12. Discussions are carried out more freely and democratically; 13. Meetings are operated more smoothly; 14. Repairs and installation of equipment and facilities are done more rationally; 15. Human relations are improved.

4. Fundamentals of QC Circle

As we have seen the QC Circle is a small group of from 5 to 10 workers who perform quality control activities voluntarily in the same workshop. Within this small group all the participating members are continuously engaged in self- and mutual-development, control and improvement, by utilizing statistical quality control techniques as a part of company-wide quality control activities.

The basic ideas behind QC Circle activities are: 1. To contribute to the improvement and development of the enterprise; 2. To respect human relations and build a happy workshop offering job satisfaction; 3. To deploy human capabilities fully and draw out infinite potential.